SA'
Alpha

BY MIKE DION
ILLUSTRATED BY
MERYL TREATNER

Celebration Press
Pearson Learning Group

CONTENTS

Chapter 1

Making Room

"Why do we have to clean out the garden shed?" asked Jason Nagawa.

He kept some things here that didn't fit in his room. Most of it was stuff about his imaginary planet, Alpha Nagawa. There were drawings; there were plans for things he wanted to build. They were stored in boxes at the back of the shed. He didn't want to take them out.

"Remember, Pop arrives tomorrow," said Mom.

Jason nodded. It wasn't just a visit—his grandfather was moving in with them for good. Jason recalled the family conference they'd had last week. Mom and Dad had explained that Pop Silva would be coming to live with them soon. Jason remembered Mom saying, "Things are going to change some. We may have to give away some things to make room. We'll all have to sacrifice a little."

"But—the garden shed?" Jason asked.

"Pop Silva wants a place where he can go sometimes for privacy," explained Dad, "a place where he can keep some things from his boat. I'm sorry, Jason, but you'll need to move your stuff, all of it."

"And if you can't find a place to put it," said Mom, "I'm afraid you'll have to give it away."

Give away the baseball cap he'd worn during the winning Little League season two years ago? No way. Give away his science fiction books, and the models he'd made of Alpha Nagawa? Out of the question!

Jason bent his lean body around the bicycles hanging on the wall of the shed. His boxes were in back, next to the pottery wheel

and the empty rabbit cage. The shed was only two feet wider than his outstretched arms, and only ten feet long.

"Pop Silva can't make a room out of this!" he objected.

No one could! The roof leaked in the back. Besides, the shed was full. It held the workbench and garden equipment, as well as the stuff Jason never wanted to throw away.

Dad shook his head. "It will have to do," he said. "This is the only extra space we have."

Although he'd been told they'd all have to give up something, Jason didn't think having to move his things out of the shed was fair. Making room for Pop had already crowded the Nagawas. Jason's big brother, Andy, had moved into Jason's bedroom. Andy now shared Jason's storage space, which meant there wasn't much left for Jason. Jason had just had to take half his stuff off his shelves and store it under his bed.

Pop would have Andy's old room. Andy was good-natured about losing his room. Jason didn't understand it. Andy said he didn't mind sharing; he'd leave for college in two years anyway. Only Jason minded.

Jason's upstairs neighbor Amy Seko joined the Nagawas at the shed door. She tried to keep her wiggling dog, Sushi, from escaping her arms.

"What's happening?" she asked.

Mom explained. Amy lived on the second floor with her mother and older brother, Craig. She and Jason went to the same school. In fact, they'd started kindergarten together. Seeing her gave Jason an idea.

"How about one of the apartments for Pop Silva?" he bargained. "He'd be in the same building with us, just on a different floor!"

Jason hoped his idea would work. The Nagawas owned their apartment house. They lived on the first floor. A single man lived on the top floor. He worked late all the time and was away most weekends. Maybe he would move out!

"No one wants to move," said Dad.

Jason heard the reproach in Dad's voice that meant Jason was being thoughtless. He knew he was asking for trouble, but he still couldn't keep quiet.

"It's too small in here!" he protested.

Sushi succeeded in wriggling out of Amy's arms. He sprinted past Jason's feet and into the shed, his backside wagging madly. He sped from place to place, sniffing.

"Pop's been a fisherman all his life," Mom said. "He's used to small spaces. Look at the inside of his fishing boats! Pop likes things small and shipshape."

"Come on, Jason, be reasonable," said Dad. "Pop Silva is family. He's all alone now, and we agreed we wanted him here with us."

Jason knew it was time to give up, but he didn't want to. "I don't see how anyone can fix up this space," he argued.

"Pop can do it," said Mom. "You'll see, because you're the one who will be helping him build. You have some extra time after school, and we expect you to pitch in every day."

"Build?" said Amy. "Can I help?"

Jason shrugged. Once Amy met Pop, she'd probably change her mind. Pop was loud and stubborn, and he never sat still—sort of like Sushi. On second thought, Amy would probably love Pop. Jason gave a short sigh.

"Why me?" he asked. "I don't know how to build stuff!"

"This is how you'll learn," said Mom in her "that's-enough" voice.

9

Jason couldn't believe it! He was the one who would have to spend the most time with Pop! Mom worked in a law office. Andy played on the varsity soccer team. When Andy didn't have practice after school, he had a game, and when he didn't have practice or a game, he worked with Dad and Grandfather Nagawa in the family import business.

When was Jason ever going to have time for Planet Nagawa? His computer game was just getting interesting! Jason had programmed the Alpha Nagawans to run around the edge of the screen so they could surround the Creature from the MegaSlime asteroid!

"Let's get going," Mom said. "We have to clean out the shed now. Your father will organize a place in the basement for the sports and garden equipment. He's already packed up some things to give to charity that we had stored there. You sort through these cartons for things to throw out or give away."

Amy helped Jason wrestle the top box to the floor. Jason opened it and peered in. He saw his drawings of Alpha Nagawa and a clay figure of Isho Mayoko, Alpha Nagawa's Peerless Leader. He'd keep those. In fact, he didn't see anything in there he wanted to throw away.

Amy took out a small wooden box and held it up, her eyebrows raised.

"That's a good box," said Jason, alarmed. "I can use it for something."

That box would make an excellent space station for the miniature creatures on Alpha Nagawa.

"You haven't used it yet," Amy pointed out.

She placed the box in the shed's trash bin. But when Jason saw that good box in the trash, he felt ill. He took it out again.

"I'll use it for pencils," he said to Amy's raised eyebrows.

Mom laughed. "It's in his genes, David," she said to Dad. "He's just like my father! Pop could never throw away a 'good little box.'"

How could Mom think he was like Pop Silva? A little tough guy with a stubborn chin and tough way of talking? Jason didn't think so.

Dad took a bicycle from its giant hook on the shed wall. "You know you can't save it all, son," he said sadly. "Some of it has to go."

Jason stuck his chin out. He felt like saying it wasn't his stuff that had to go; it was Pop Silva. Did he really mean that, though? Would he choose a wooden box over a grandfather?

Maybe.

Chapter 2

A Reprieve

Andy ran up, all strong and energetic, and began to move things out of the shed.

"Hi, Bug!" he said to Amy in his cheerful voice. "Watch you don't get squashed!"

"You!" said Amy scornfully. "You must take brother lessons from Craig!"

Andy laughed. He grabbed two shrub trimmers from the wall and followed Mom and Dad to the basement.

"Hey, Jason," said Amy, "why not put all the Alpha Nagawa stuff in one box and throw away the rest?"

Jason groaned. "I don't want to throw anything away!" he said. "But my room is pretty full—two dressers, two beds, two computers!"

"I have an idea!" exclaimed Amy. "Maybe you could put your stuff in our storage space!"

Jason brightened. The tenants each had a locked storage compartment in the basement. It would be great if he could store his boxes in the Sekos' space!

"That would be awesome!" he said.

"I'll go get the key," said Amy. Then she grabbed Sushi and took off.

Jason turned back to his boxes. He wasn't sure why his parents were so anxious to have Pop Silva move out to San Francisco anyway. Pop had never paid them much attention that Jason could see. The Nagawas had visited Grandma and Pop Silva in Bedford, Massachusetts, every few summers. But Pop had been to San Francisco only twice that Jason remembered.

Jason had liked when Grandma Silva visited. She was loud, too, but she liked to laugh. She reminded Jason of Mom.

Pop Silva never laughed; he only worked. He weeded the garden. He painted the basement door yellow without checking with anyone.

The last time Jason saw Pop was last year, at Grandma Silva's funeral. Pop was practically a stranger. Jason knew his other grandparents, who lived nearby, much better.

Jason pulled a few things out of the open box. He carried them up to the apartment and into his room. He tried to fit his stack of drawings of Alpha Nagawa under his bed; no go. He had to squeeze them into his box of computer games. He put the three books he'd made in school last year, all about adventures on Alpha Nagawa, on his bedside table.

Someone knocked on the kitchen door. Now what?

"Are you in there?" called Amy. "I've got the key!"

They took the inside stairs down to the basement. Mom and Dad and Andy were down there already, organizing things. The basement was now almost as full as the shed had been—two washers, two dryers, the new workbench, and the garden equipment.

Amy ran to unlock the Sekos' storage compartment. Jason stretched to pull the chain for the overhead light, and his hopes fell. The Sekos' storage space was beyond full.

"Oh, I forgot about my aunt," said Amy. She looked at Jason apologetically. "We're storing her furniture while she's away at graduate school."

By now Jason and Amy had caught the family's attention.

"Using Amy's storage space is cheating!" Andy called. He had a laugh in his voice.

"Jason," said Dad reproachfully.

"I'm desperate, Dad!" said Jason. "I just can't throw away my stuff this fast!"

Dad relented. "Okay," he said. "I'll give you a little more time. You can leave your boxes in the basement for now."

"Thanks, Dad!" said Jason.

A temporary solution was better than none at all.

Chapter 3

POP ARRIVES

Pop Silva threw another shingle off the roof of the shed. Jason winced. This situation was worse than he had thought it would be. Pop Silva hadn't been here 24 hours, and already he had the roof of the garden shed half off!

Pop had started to work the minute he saw the shed.

"First we re-roof," he announced in his gruff voice. "Then we set in windows. Then we insulate. Then we put up new inside walls, all wood, just like my boat. No problem."

"No problem" was Pop Silva's favorite phrase. He said it every time he tore something apart.

"What should we do?" Jason asked Mom when the first roof shingle hit the ground. That was about 20 minutes after Pop arrived.

"Laugh," advised Mom.

More shingles hit the grass.

"Help him," suggested Dad.

So they all helped—Mom and Dad, Andy
and Jason. They were still working when
Grandmother and Grandfather Nagawa came
for dinner. Grandmother Nagawa shook her
head. Grandfather Nagawa joined in to help.

Grandfather and Grandmother Nagawa lived
only a block away, in the ground-floor
apartment of a building like the one Jason's
dad and mom owned. They had a garden shed,
too, but theirs held only garden equipment.

Grandfather Nagawa owned an import business with Dad. They had two stores and a warehouse, and they shipped their goods all over the United States.

Mom and Grandmother Nagawa went inside to cook dinner. Jason knew that Grandmother Nagawa didn't know what to make of Pop Silva. Pop hadn't come down from the ladder when she arrived. He'd just shouted "Hello!" and kept on working. Grandmother wouldn't say anything, though. She wanted to make Pop Silva feel welcome.

Jason and Andy kept working while Mom and Grandmother cooked. When dinner was ready, they had to serve it in the backyard to get Pop Silva to eat anything. Mom made Pop sit down with them at the picnic table to eat Grandmother's special shrimp dish. Pop ate it in what seemed to Jason about five seconds.

"Good!" he commented. "Thanks!"

Then he was up and running. By the time darkness came, Pop Silva had the flashing and tar paper laid down on the shed roof. Life with Pop would not be quiet, Jason decided.

Chapter 4

A Big Problem

Jason woke Monday morning to the sound of hammering. A glance out the window revealed Pop Silva, kneeling on the shed roof pounding nails into the new roof shingles.

"His back!" groaned Mom. "He's not supposed to fish anymore because of his back, and look at him!"

Jason couldn't see that there was anything wrong with Pop's back.

"I guess you can't teach an old dog new tricks," said Dad.

Jason left for school. He was glad to go. He forgot about Pop for most of the day. Then he remembered that he was expected to help Pop after school. When he and Amy got home, they were just in time to watch Pop cut a hole in the wall of the shed to make a window opening.

Amy was fascinated.

"I'll be right back!" she said.

She left Jason in the backyard with Pop and rushed up to her apartment for Sushi. She was back in a flash, eager to watch Pop work. Jason could see that Pop loved being watched. He also loved giving orders.

"Hand me that level," he said.

Pop held his hand out without looking at either Amy or Jason. Amy and Sushi rushed to obey. Jason made a face. He didn't want any part of this. He was starving, and he had homework. Most of all he wanted to get to his boxes and sort out his stuff.

But there was no polite way Jason could get into the house; he had agreed to help. He and Amy handed Pop tools and picked up debris. Pop Silva didn't take breaks. Not content that one window had been cut, he had to cut another.

"If one window is good, two are better!"
said Pop.

Jason sneered. Was that a joke? Amy laughed.

"No problem!" Pop told Amy. "One more
window to frame! Insulation is next!"

"No problem, no problem," Jason mimicked
in his head. "No problem, that is, except Pop."

"Look at that!" said Pop proudly when he'd
finished cutting the hole for the second
window. "Two windows!"

Amy and Sushi looked at the new window opening with admiration. Jason looked away, focusing on the stack of wood that would be Pop's inside walls. Dad had tried to talk Pop into using plasterboard, saying that wood walls would be too dark, but Pop Silva just shook his head.

"Wood," he'd insisted. "Like my boat."

"Help him buy the wood, David," said Mom. "Pop has his mind made up."

Amy's mother came home from work. She called for Amy and Sushi to come in. Jason's stomach growled. Maybe Pop would stop now.

But Pop muttered something about framing one of his new windows. He asked Jason to plug the table saw into the electrical outlet for him. Pop sawed a piece of framing. Then he went into the shed and held the framing up to a window opening. Jason started for the house and food, but Pop stopped him.

"Hammer," snapped Pop, holding out his hand.

He didn't even look at Jason. Jason suddenly felt very angry and hurt. Who did Pop think he was? But Jason picked up the hammer.

"Here it is," he said as politely as possible. He did not put the hammer into Pop's hand; he set it nearby carefully. Then he took off.

"Hey!" called Pop. "Where are you going?"

No, no way! Enough was enough! Jason thudded up the back steps. He let the back door slam, breaking an apartment-house rule. He'd just had it with Pop Silva.

Jason invented an excuse as he flew out the front door. He had to get to the library to research a paper on Alzheimer's disease—that was it. It was a lie, but he needed the peace and quiet, no matter what the consequences.

Chapter 5

Consequences

The consequences were horrible. Jason didn't make it back home before Mom returned from work, so she knew he'd disobeyed and had been gone. She was no happier when he told her his lie about needing to do some library research. She made him apologize to Pop Silva. For some reason Pop wouldn't look at him.

But the worst consequence came when Dad got home and heard the story. "You've lost the extra time I gave you, Jason. You'll need to decide which things you want to keep. Tomorrow I'm delivering all our boxes to charity," said Dad.

Jason's heart pounded. "But—" he stammered.

"No arguments," said Dad.

"Smart move, Alien," murmured Andy.

"Alien" was Andy's pet name for Jason, thanks to Jason's long-time love of science fiction.

"I had to go to the library!" protested Jason.

"Right," said Andy.

Jason felt his face burn. Andy could always tell when he lied.

"Next time wait and go after dinner," said Mom.

"Or you can start your research on the Internet," said Andy helpfully.

"I know," muttered Jason.

He sent a sidelong glance at Pop. Pop still wasn't looking at him.

"Do you have a computer, Pop?" he asked.

"Had radar on the boat," said Pop. "Helped me find the fish."

But he still wouldn't look at Jason. There was a long uncomfortable silence.

"Pop's crates came today," said Andy, trying to change the subject. "Imagine, seven crates full of Pop's stuff!"

Now Jason couldn't look at Pop. He couldn't keep his boxes, but Pop had seven crates! This day got worse and worse.

"Seven crates!" said Jason.

"I think it's pretty good to be able to get a lifetime's worth of belongings into seven crates," said Dad.

He smiled at Pop Silva.

"What more do I need?" said Pop.

He didn't smile back, though. He just looked forlorn. Jason felt worse and worse.

Dinner was uncomfortable and homework was hard. Jason couldn't concentrate. His mind wandered to Alpha Nagawa. There were no fights on Alpha Nagawa. Well, there were fights between the Alpha Nagawans and unfriendly space aliens. But all the Alpha Nagawans liked the same things.

Alpha Nagawans liked to play Float Soccer. Players kicked a Planet Nagawa rock. It floated for a while before it landed. If it landed in a crater, the player scored a point.

Alpha Nagawans liked to ride their Tri-Comets. A Tri-Comet looked like a Ferris wheel car on a triangular base. Hydrogen was its fuel. It could take riders anywhere very fast, but only in a zigzag line.

Each Alpha Nagawan also had an underground hideaway. The hideaways could branch in any direction. Jason drew them to look like the inside of an anthill, or an upside-down treehouse. Alpha Nagawans kept their treasures in their hideaways.

Jason knew what he would keep in his. He'd have bits of glittery meteors. He'd have a colony of the tiny singing bugs that lived on Alpha Nagawa. He'd have a collection of space jetsam that landed on Alpha Nagawa from other planets.

Andy's computer beeped, and Jason came back from Planet Nagawa. His mind strayed to his boxes down in the basement. The Alpha Nagawa Communications Center was in one of those boxes. Jason had spent an entire summer building the Communications Center. Everyone helped—Amy, Andy, Dad, and even Grandfather Nagawa.

Painted cardboard Alpha Nagawans clustered at a long control panel in front of a long wall. Three different buttons lit three different sets of lights. Another button made a siren go off. The lights were the tiny ones for Christmas trees. The siren came from Andy's old train set.

Jason gave up on homework. He stole through the kitchen and into the back hall. He opened the door to the basement stairs. He hoped none of the other tenants were down there, doing their laundry.

The basement was quiet. Jason flipped a switch. A double row of light bulbs glowed from their cords like weak suns. They lit up someone's laundry—the Sekos', guessed Jason. He recognized Amy's red sweatshirt hanging on the washline.

Jason found the Alpha Nagawa
Communications Center in the second box.
He lifted it out carefully. The blue, silver, and
bright yellow paint glinted, even in the poor
light. Jason wanted to keep it, but he didn't
have space in his room. He was afraid to ask
Dad now if he could keep it. He knew he
would still be too angry to agree. He knew
Mom would never say yes unless Jason had
room for it.

"Really got you in trouble, didn't I?" came a
gruff voice.

Jason started.

"Pop?" he said.

"Yeah. I couldn't sleep; I felt bad."

Jason watched Pop's bare feet come farther down the basement stairs. Pants legs followed the feet. A T-shirt followed the pants legs, then Pop's head. Pop's gray hair sprayed out above his ears and made a ring around the middle of his bald, suntanned head. Soon all of Pop stood barefoot on the cement floor.

Pop was little, but he towered. What did he want? Did he want Jason to apologize again?

Jason licked his dry lips.

"I shouldn't have just taken off," he told Pop. "I didn't even have to go to the library."

"I shouldn't have worked you to death," replied Pop. "You're a boy, just a boy."

Jason flushed. He wanted to say, "You're just an old man!" But he bit his tongue. He'd learned his lesson, the one about acting on impulse.

"Anyway, sorry I got you in trouble," said Pop. "You have to get rid of all your stuff, huh?"

Jason nodded.

"Because I'm taking the space where you used to store it, right?"

Jason nodded again.

"That isn't right," said Pop. "But they're your parents, and what they say goes. Tell you what, though. I'll store some of your things in my new room if you want. You can go in any time to get them, whether I'm there or not."

Jason didn't know if he wanted to do that or not, but it felt good that Pop had offered.

"Thanks," he said.

"What's that thing?" asked Pop, nodding at the model Jason held.

Jason showed him the Communications Center. Pop took it in his own hands and looked it over, front and back. Then he set it on the workbench and plugged it in. He pushed the buttons. The lights came on. The siren wailed.

"Guess I'm going to have to learn more about Planet Nagawa," was all he said.

Chapter 6

RESCUED TREASURES

Jason had to get up early to finish his homework. Amy called for him when it was time for school, but Jason couldn't go with her. Dad made him load his boxes into the back of the van. Then Dad drove him to school.

Jason could feel his boxes behind him the whole way. Everything inside those boxes cried out "Save me!" Jason tried not to think about the treasures he was losing. He stuck out his jaw. He would not let Dad see him cry. At least Dad took him to school first, so Jason didn't have to go along to give away the boxes.

As Jason and Amy walked home from school together that afternoon, Jason brought her up to date on everything. Amy's eyes got wider and wider.

"Oh, boy," she said. "You really got in trouble!"

"Yeah," said Jason.

"Your grandfather was pretty nice, though, about storing the Communications Center for you."

"Yeah," said Jason again.

He wondered whether he should tell Amy the other nice thing he suspected about Pop. One of the boxes he'd loaded into Dad's van that morning felt awfully light. Maybe Pop Silva had saved something else!

Jason decided not to tell Amy. He didn't want to say it out loud and get his hopes up. Maybe it wasn't true.

"I'm going to grab something to eat," said Jason when they reached their apartment building. "Then I'm going right out back to help Pop with the shed. You coming?"

"Sure!" said Amy.

Jason waited while she ran upstairs to get Sushi. Then they went out back.

It was too quiet out here. Jason hoped Pop was all right.

"How's the work going?" called Amy.

"Windows," came Pop's voice.

The voice was still gruff, but it was too quiet. Jason saw that one of the windows was in place now. Jason wanted to hear the old Pop again, loud and energetic. He tried teasing him.

"Pop!" he said. "Aren't you finished with both windows yet?"

Now Pop came to the door of the shed.

"My back," he said, no smile.

Jason reminded himself that Pop didn't get jokes. Pop's tired face worried him.

"What's next?" he asked. "Insulation?" He tried to sound cheerful, like Andy.

"I think I just want to take a look at my stuff," said Pop. "See if it got here okay."

He nodded behind him. Jason peered into the shed. He saw a broom, sawdust swept into a pile, and two good-sized wooden crates. Sushi sat on top of one of them.

"Did you carry those out, Pop?" asked Amy.

"Yeah," said Pop. "Stupid old man, huh?"

Jason silently agreed. No wonder Pop's back hurt.

"You're not stupid," said Amy loyally.

"I'd want to see if my stuff got here okay, too," said Jason. "But that's how you hurt your back, I'll bet."

Pop nodded. "Next time I'll wait till your brother gets home."

"He can lift anything," agreed Amy.

"At least I can pry a crate open for you," said Jason. "Which one do you want to open first?"

Pop nodded at one of the crates. He sat next to Sushi on the other one. Sushi hopped up on his lap.

Amy gave Pop a worried glance.

"I'm going to make us some iced tea," she said. "Okay?"

Pop didn't answer. Now Jason was worried.

"Sounds great to me, Amy," Jason said. "Right, Pop?"

Pop nodded, but Jason could tell Pop wasn't really paying attention. His eyes were fixed on the crate.

"I'll be back soon," said Amy.

She called to Sushi. Instead of obeying, Sushi flopped down on Pop's lap and yawned.

"He's all right here," said Pop.

"Okay," said Amy, "if you're sure." She took off.

Jason began to pry the top off the crate.

"Where did you get this?" he asked Pop. "It's a great box."

"Made it," said Pop.

"Wow," said Jason. He was beginning to think Pop could build anything.

"It had to be strong, see," said Pop. "I wanted my things to get here in one piece. I couldn't trust anyone else to do it right."

Now Jason was really curious. What was so important to Pop that he made these crates to ship it in?

Jason got to work. Pop had used long nails to hold the top in place. It took all Jason's strength to pull them loose. Finally he lifted the top.

Together Pop and Jason peered into the crate. Jason saw a set of small cupboards, some old varnished boards, and some small wire racks.

"What's all this stuff?" he asked.

"Parts of the *Louisa*," said Pop. "I may not be able to fish anymore, but I couldn't just leave the *Louisa* behind."

Jason's jaw dropped. He knew Pop had had three fishing boats over time. All of them had been named the *Louisa*, after Grandma Silva.

"No kidding?" said Jason. "Are you going to use this stuff here, in the shed?"

Pop Silva nodded.

"Pull out that cupboard, will you, Jason?" he asked. "My back's got a twinge. I know we're not ready to put up cupboards yet; we need walls first. I just want to try it out, see where it might fit."

Carefully Jason pulled out the small cupboard unit. The wood was mahogany, he thought, or maybe teak—boat wood. It smelled of salt, and it shone like satin. It shone like pearls. It shone

like the sun on the sea! The Alpha Nagawans would recognize it as a great treasure. Jason loved it.

"So you like to save things, too, huh Pop?" asked Jason.

Pop nodded. "I made that set of cupboards for the first *Louisa*. When I sold her, I took the cupboards out and put them in the second *Louisa*."

"But you just took these out of the third *Louisa*, right?" asked Jason.

"Yes, I did," said Pop.

"Did you sell the second *Louisa,* too?" asked Jason.

Pop's face clouded over.

"No," he said. "She got broken up in a bad storm. A hurricane will do that sometimes— come in and smash everything, just like a bad-tempered child. I had to work awhile on other people's boats before I got the third *Louisa*. She was the best of the lot. I had her 15 years."

Jason could tell he missed her. Maybe he missed her as much as he missed Grandma Silva. It would be hard to lose your wife and the boat you loved all in the same year. It would be harder to lose all that than to lose a few boxes. After all, Jason still had Alpha Nagawa.

Jason looked around the shed. Fixing up the shed was sort of like making up Alpha Nagawa. You got an idea, and you tried it out. Maybe he and Pop Silva were alike after all. They both liked to build their own places.

Pop handed Jason the cupboard.

"Hold this up over by the door," he said.

Pop was ordering him around again! Pop Silva was back! Jason grinned. He held the cupboard up next to the door. Pop cocked his head.

"Looks good there," he said. "Maybe that's where I'll put it. We'll see after the walls are up."

Jason's arms began to ache. He put the cupboard down.

"I brought two more cupboards," said Pop. "Maybe you can use one for your Planet Alpha Nagawa stuff. Or maybe we can build a cabinet for it."

Maybe this was going to work out after all, having Pop here! Jason took a deep breath.

"Pop," he said, "About my boxes—"

"Your boxes," said Pop. "Well, I hope you don't mind, but I got sort of interested in this planet stuff."

He bent over the toolbox and came up with a fat sketchbook. Jason's heart gave a leap. It was his notebook! His plans! His ideas about Alpha Nagawa!

"This looked to me like a ship's log," said Pop. "So when I taped your box up again, I kept it out."

"Awesome!" cried Jason.

He leaped for the notebook. Sushi got excited and leaped, too.

47

"Looked pretty interesting," said Pop. He picked up the set of cupboards and held it up to the wall. "You can build some stuff you planned and drew in your sketchbook right into a cabinet in the shed if you like," he said, without looking at Jason. Jason *would* like that—a lot.

"Is it hard?" Jason asked.

"Nothing to it," replied Pop. He shifted the cabinet. "Yes, sir, it will be good to have part of my boat here."

Jason knew just how Pop felt. "I hope when this shed is finished, it makes you feel right at home," Jason said.

He meant it, too.